Barbara Hepworth

Sculpture Garden

3

730.92 HEP

Barbara Hepworth
Sculpture Garden, St Ives

Miranda Phillips
and Chris Stephens

Tate Publishing

First published 2002 by order of the Tate Trustees
by Tate Publishing, a division of Tate Enterprises Ltd,
Millbank, London SW1P 4RG

www.tate.org.uk

British Library Cataloguing in Publication Data
A catalogue record for this book is available from the British Library

ISBN 1 85437 412 5

Distributed in North and South America by
Harry N. Abrams, Inc., New York,
under the following ISBN:
ISBN 0-8109-6255-1

Library of Congress Cataloging in Publication Data
Library of Congress Control Number: 2002104380

FRONT COVER
View of *Two Forms (Divided Circle)* by Barbara Hepworth in March, with *Euryops pectinatus* in the foreground

BACK COVER
Barbara Hepworth in Trewyn Studio garden,
April 1970

FRONTISPIECE
Barbara Hepworth in Trewyn Studio garden,
15 May 1970

ACKNOWLEDGEMENTS
John Anderson, Bob Berry, Sir Alan Bowness, Brian Smith.
Thanks also to Peter B. Evans.

PHOTOGRAPHIC CREDITS
All the photographs in this publication were taken by Bob Berry and are © Tate Enterprises, except the following:
pp.2, 7, 11, 15, 19 © Alan Bowness, Hepworth Estate
back cover, pp.8 Tate Gallery Archive
pp.17 Tate Gallery Archive, photo: Crispin Purich
pp.29, 30 bottom, 39 Tate Gallery Photographic Department

DESIGNED BY
Groundwork, Skipton

PRINTED BY
Snoeck-Ducaju & Zoon, Gent, Belgium

Contents

'A Sort of Magic'

Chris Stephens

'Finding Trewyn Studio was a sort of magic', Barbara Hepworth wrote of her St Ives studio.[1] Halfway up a steep, cobbled hill, hidden above the heads of passers-by behind high retaining walls, Trewyn Studio and its garden seemed then, as now, a secret haven amongst the tightly-packed houses and crowded narrow streets of old St Ives. There, for twenty-five years, Hepworth and her team of assistants produced sculptures in wood, stone, metal and plaster for bronze. As Trewyn became an attraction for collectors and critics from around the world, the garden was drawn into the presentation and reception of the artist's public image. Though essentially a private space, this was not simply a back garden, nor even a working yard, but an essential part of Hepworth's creative process and of the message she wished to convey with her sculpture. Hepworth's garden helped to secure the association of her apparently abstract works with the natural world. Its exotic planting and location in west Cornwall, with its sub-tropical climate and clear light, served to link her to a Mediterranean sensibility that was in contrast to orthodox British culture.

During the 1940s Hepworth had worked at Chy-an-Kerris, the home in nearby Carbis Bay that she shared with Ben Nicholson and their three children. This restricted both the number and size of sculptures she could produce and caused inevitable tensions between her roles as a wife and mother and as an independent artist. In 1949 her attention was drawn to the forthcoming sale of Trewyn Studio. The building and garden had, at one time, belonged to the large Trewyn House next door. With her growing reputation and increasingly strained family relations, she recognised the importance of the place, and with financial assistance from Nicholson's old supporter Helen Sutherland, Hepworth went to the auction with her close friend Marcus Brumwell to bid on her behalf. 'The first bid was far beyond my figure,' she recalled, 'and, according to my friends, I went pale green and fainted – so the bidding went on and I got the place … there I was – space, air, sun and a real proper workshop. The children had their own quarters just opposite and Ben his own big studio, and we all began to expand and grow.'[2] Though originally intended as a place purely for work, within a year Trewyn became Hepworth's home when divisions in the family proved irreparable and she and Nicholson separated and eventually divorced. Despite her growing fame and affluence, Hepworth remained in this modest studio until her tragic death in a fire there in May 1975.

[1] *Barbara Hepworth: A Pictorial Autobiography*, London 1970, rev. ed. 1978, p.52

[2] Ibid.

Barbara Hepworth standing next to *Figure (Archaean)* in Trewyn Studio garden, August 1962

3 John Anderson, 'Barbara Hepworth's Garden', *The Cornish Garden*, no.34, March 1991, p.24

4 Brian Smith, letter to the author, 29 June 1998

5 Brian Smith recalls twenty-six works in the garden that are no longer there, but some of these were removed during Hepworth's lifetime

It is unclear now how much of the present garden was already laid out when Hepworth moved to Trewyn in 1949. As part of the grounds to the big house, it was certainly cultivated, and some of the existing trees were already in place. Many others she planted herself, including a magnificent magnolia, copper beech, oak, holly, pear and flowering cherry. Photographs from the early 1950s suggest a rectilinear plan already interspersed with sculptures.[3] In 1965 an extra strip of land, at the top of the garden, was purchased from the sculptor John Milne, then the occupant of Trewyn House. Shortly before Hepworth's death, a further small area was acquired to accommodate the multi-part *Conversation with Magic Stones* (1973).

How Hepworth conceived the relationship between the garden and her sculpture is uncertain. According to her secretary, Brian Smith, the place was not intended to be a 'sculpture garden' for public use, and though a visiting collector might be invited to stroll around, Hepworth rarely sold work from it. This was 'her own private garden with examples of her own work for her own enjoyment'.[4] Plants were chosen according to the artist's preference, though they also complemented the sculptures. Foliage was important as it provided a good background to the works. The style of the sculptures' presentation was simple – they were erected on the easily-moveable breezeblock piles on which she sometimes carved. How deliberately they were sited is also subject to question. It is most likely that she took considerable care over this in the early days, but practical factors may have impinged upon the overall design. From 1956, Hepworth cast more works in bronze than she made unique carvings. As each bronze edition included an additional cast reserved for the artist, the number of works needing a home greatly increased. In 1960, she acquired the former Palais de Danse across the road to provide extra storage as well as additional working space. Nevertheless, several stone carvings stayed in the garden and Hepworth seems to have tended to place larger bronzes there too. From the mid-1960s, poor health – including cancer and a broken hip that caused lasting pain – hampered her mobility and management of the studio. This, perhaps, was one reason why the sculptures in the garden accumulated. While the pieces we see now are generally where they were placed in her lifetime, before the garden opened to the public numerous works were removed,[5] including her *Family of Man* (1970), a group of nine man-size

CHRIS STEPHENS

Barbara Hepworth carving *Contrapuntal Forms*
in 1950

totemic figures. This gives some indication of how over-crowded the place had become.

As well as a garden, this was also a working space. As soon as Hepworth acquired Trewyn, two huge blocks of limestone, which would eventually stand as *Contrapuntal Forms* beside the Dome of Discovery at the 1951 Festival of Britain, were positioned in the small concrete patch in front of a shed. Her turntable, with blocks of marble waiting to be carved, now indicates how carving continued there until her death. In the early days she carved wood in the studio and worked on stone alongside her assistants in the garden. In 1957 a large shed was rebuilt as a workshop, which is now preserved largely as it was left at her death. The assistants' overalls – each had their own colour – hang on the door, while an array of points, claws, hammers and rasps gives a sense of how the stone was worked. It was only late in life that Hepworth allowed the limited use of power-tools. Next door, the plaster workshop is dominated by an unfinished cast of the wooden sculpture *Oval Form (Delos)* of 1955. Fragments of other works can also be seen: against the back wall the plaster for *Maquette (Variation on a Theme)* – a work related to *Garden Sculpture (Model for Meridian)* (1958) outside – stands to the right; to the left of the mirror are stacked plasters for three forms that were designed for the exterior of the John Lewis department store in London's Oxford Street but never used (a maquette is in the house). Unfinished pieces demonstrate how the plaster was applied to a chicken-wire armature, modelled when wet and then carved and smoothed when dry. Though they were occasionally exhibited, plasters were not seen as works in their own right but as models from which an edition of bronzes would be cast. In the top greenhouse are three plasters – *Sea Form (Porthmeor)* (1958), *Square Forms (Two Sequences)* (1963–4) and *The Family of Man, Figure 8: The Bride* (1970) – two of which were exhibited, which may be why they are painted to look like bronze.

The juxtaposition of the plasters with the collection of cacti highlights a point of obvious formal comparison. Hepworth's work was, essentially, linked to nature: either its shape might have derived from a natural form or, more conceptually, it may have been determined by an idea of the organic, of growth or form. In this way, several of the sculptures in the garden – *Corymb*, say, or *Meridian* – integrate themselves with the flowers and bushes around them. Though it became more dominant from the 1940s, this organic aesthetic had always been an aspect of Hepworth's art. Similarly, she had long sited sculptures out-of-doors. Two large works of the 1930s were positioned in gardens in Hampstead – her own and that of the artist, writer and collector Roland Penrose; both were damaged by wartime bombing. During the war, Hepworth photographed sculptures – her own and those of Naum Gabo – against the backdrop of St Ives Bay, radically repositioning their constructivist aesthetic. After the war, however, this dialogue between art work and nature came to the fore. Though she aspired to siting works in the landscape (as Henry Moore managed to do), the garden at Trewyn became the principal location for this exchange, as the forms and textures of plants and sculptures provided a complement and a counterpoint to each other.

Hepworth used her situation in Trewyn in the presentation of her work to the public. Many of her sculptures were photographed with evocative backgrounds. The most notable example is an image of the artist reaching up in the dawn half-light to finish off the plaster for *Cantate Domino* (which translates as 'Sing unto the Lord') against a backdrop of the tower of the parish church. Some works appear monumental set against the rooftops of St Ives; others are integrated with the sea-view. Thus, Hepworth's home and workplace became tied up with her public image as an artist. This became especially true in the early 1960s, when catalogues and articles included photographs of the artist seated in the garden surrounded by her work. Now there are only a few stone sculptures in the garden and the majority are bronze. Then, when she was new to metal casts, the display was a range of stones of different colours, textures and densities. Surrounded by foliage, it might have looked as if these were some sort of early monoliths emerging from the landscape. Hepworth's friend, the critic J.P. Hodin, identified one material in particular that resonated with this special location and linked the sculptor to a more exotic place: white marble. He wrote:

> We were sitting in the garden of Barbara Hepworth's Trewyn Studio. It was a late afternoon in the summer, the sky was blue, the bells of the nearby church sounded clear in the warm air … one could hear from afar the mighty roar of the waves … Under palm trees and flowering shrubs, between roses and gladioli some work of this outstanding English sculptor stood in the open. Nowhere in England had the spirit of the Mediterranean embodied itself so generously …

View of Trewyn Studio garden in summer

I remarked that we might be sitting in Greece or in Southern Italy …
so unmistakeably classical was the marble, the light and the sound of
the South.[6]

Though she later realised that marble cannot be kept out of doors in the British climate, Hepworth concurred:

I love marble specially because of its radiance in the light, its
hardness, precision and response to the sun. All this I learned to
appreciate in Italy when I was a young student, and to have found
this spot in Cornwall where nature corresponds so genuinely to my
concept of style and my whole feeling has for years been a deep
source of joy and satisfaction.[7]

Trewyn Studio and its garden provided the private space in which Hepworth was able to produce an extraordinary body of work. Almost inevitably, the garden and sculpture became locked into a creative dialogue. Just as that integration of art with nature created a peaceful environment for the artist, so it has helped to secure her posthumous reputation.

[6] J.P. Hodin, 'Barbara Hepworth and the
Mediterranean Spirit', *Marmo*, no.3,
December 1964, p.59

[7] Ibid.

Denis Mitchell, Barbara Hepworth and John Wells at
work on *Contrapuntal Forms*, Trewyn Studio, 1950

Trewyn Studio – Barbara Hepworth's Garden in St Ives

Miranda Phillips

When Barbara Hepworth came to Cornwall in August 1939 she could little have thought that she would spend the rest of her life in the area. She and her husband, the painter Ben Nicholson, had left London hurriedly as the threat of war and of the bombing of the capital drew closer. They were particularly anxious for the safety of their three young children, triplets Simon, Sarah and Rachel. Initially staying with friends Adrian Stokes and Margaret Mellis at their home in Carbis Bay, just outside St Ives, Hepworth and Nicholson quickly moved into the first of two houses they rented in Carbis Bay during the war years. Through this period of hardship and self-reliance, Hepworth's determination and capacity for hard physical work were devoted to providing for her family. At first she worked in the Stokes' market garden; later, at Dunluce, their first rented house, she ran a small nursery school which allowed her to earn a little, provide a service and educate her children. Hepworth turned the garden over to vegetables during the wartime 'Dig for Victory' campaign and was awarded a local certificate for the quality of her produce. The soil in the area was fertile and free draining, and she learnt rapidly which plants would thrive and which would prove less successful. Ben reported in letters to friends that Barbara had harvested more than 600 tomatoes and an exceptional crop of Brussels sprouts in the first six months.[1] In 1942 they took a seven-year lease on a larger house, Chy-an-Kerris. Here, at last, was extra living space for a growing family. There was even a garage where Hepworth could set up a studio, but family commitments meant that her time for sculpture was severely limited. Although she did not transform the garden into a vegetable plot, she had already developed a valuable working knowledge of horticulture, on which she drew to transform the garden of her next, and final home.

Towards the end of their lease on Chy-an-Kerris, Hepworth and Nicholson began to look for separate studio and living spaces within St Ives. Throughout 1948 the local newspaper, the *St Ives Times*, reported St Ives Town Council's proposal to purchase Trewyn House and its estate, and it may have been the public outcry generated that first alerted Barbara to Trewyn Studio, which was built on the eastern end of the Trewyn House estate.[2] The Council planned to turn the gardens and orchard into a public car park, and it was this that caused the most objections. In March 1948 the issue was resolved shortly after the Council's Compulsory

[1] Sarah Jane Checkland, *Ben Nicholson*, London 2000

[2] Trewyn House (then known as 'Halse's Court') was built by James Halse, solicitor, mine adventurer and member of parliament for St Ives. He also built the village of Halsetown, close to St Ives, to house his mineworkers and their families. 'Trewyn', a Cornish word, translates as 'the fair place' or 'the place of innocence'

[3] Now Trewyn Public Gardens. Both Hepworth and John Milne later donated plants for this garden

[4] W.H. Lane and Son, auction notice, September 1949. The description recognises that suitable premises were saleable to artists. The garden is behind the Studio and greenhouse, not in front

[5] *Barbara Hepworth*, exh. cat., Marlborough-Gerson Gallery, New York 1966

Two Forms (Divided Circle) in spring

Purchase Order was refused on appeal to the Department of the Environment. The Council for the Protection of Rural England offered £25 towards buying local plants for a new public garden on the site through their local representative, Will Arnold-Forster.[3] The remaining two-thirds of the estate – Trewyn House and some mature garden and the smaller Trewyn Studio with its small garden area – were to be sold at public auction.

Hepworth had often walked past the high granite walls of Trewyn with her shopping, unaware of the hidden studio and garden within. The auction notice described the property as a 'stonebuilt studio premises and garden (of particular interest to artists and others) 30' 3" × 21' 9" [9.2 × 6.6 metres], having store and two wc's underneath, with two separate entrances. Attractive front Rose Garden with lean-to Greenhouse and store.'[4] Hepworth's move to Trewyn Studio marked the start of an entirely new way of living, for at last she had the time, space and peace required to devote her considerable energy to sculpture. The children were at boarding school for most of the year, Nicholson acquired a studio no more than five minutes walk away, and Trewyn Studio, with its high surrounding walls, offered privacy yet stood within the busy artists' community of St Ives.

Part of Hepworth's philosophy as an artist was 'to infuse the formal perfection of geometry with the vital grace of nature', and, with her abiding love of landscape, she had always drawn inspiration from the natural world.[5] Photographs of her Hampstead studio before the war show potted plants among the sculptures; many years later, pictures taken in her St Ives studio show the same casual integration of plants and works in progress. Soon after Trewyn Studio became her home, Hepworth added plants to her working environment. A set of photographs from 1950 illustrate this: terracotta pots overflowing with lemon-scented pelargoniums share shelf space with files and chisels; crassulas (jade plants) and house-leeks contrast with blocks of marble.

For the first few years there was no spare time to spend on the garden, which was used more as a stoneyard than as a place of beauty and recreation. Hepworth worked on two major commissions for the Festival of Britain of 1951, rigging up spotlights and a canvas shelter so that she could continue carving the massive blocks of stone well

MIRANDA PHILLIPS

The pond at Trewyn in March, with water hawthorn (*Aponogeton distachyos*)

6 John Milne was a former assistant of Hepworth's, later a sculptor in his own right. Trewyn House was owned by Professor Cosmo Rodewald; Milne lived there from the mid-1950s until his death in June 1978

7 Rainier purchased a small property in St Ives – Tregenna Steps Studio – in the early 1960s, dividing her time between St Ives and London, where she taught at the Royal Academy of Music. June Opie's book *'Come and Listen to the Stars Singing': Priaulx Rainier – A Pictorial Biography*, Penzance 1988, cites excerpts from Rainier's garden diary such as notes of flowering dates and bird and wildlife observations

8 All copies of Hepworth's letters and legal documents quoted here are from the St Ives Trust Archive Study Centre

9 Will Arnold-Forster, *Shrubs for the Milder Counties*, London 1948, reprinted Penzance 2000. Hepworth's copy is now owned by Sophie Bowness

10 June Opie, *'Come and Listen to the Stars Singing': Priaulx Rainier – A Pictorial Biography*, Penzance 1988, p.67

into the night. Frequently working nine-hour days, Hepworth and her assistants left the overgrown rose-beds and lawn neatly clipped but otherwise ignored.

In the mid-1950s, having produced a substantial body of work during her first few years at Trewyn Studio, Hepworth took stock of the garden. Facing south-east, it was an irregular square, sloping gently upwards to the fence and low, crumbling wall that separated it from the grounds of Trewyn House. Several mature trees and some overgrown shrubs sheltered the southern edge of the plot. The lawn was scrubby and worn, and roses bloomed raggedly, dropping their petals amongst tangles of purple and blue cinerarias. Hepworth entered negotiations with her neighbour at Trewyn House, John Milne, and they agreed to redraw the boundary 'in a straight line instead of a curved line'.[6] A document to this effect was signed in December 1956, witnessed by the painter Alan Lowndes and the composer Priaulx Rainier.[7] Hepworth's accompanying letter explained that Denis Mitchell could draw the boundary with string that afternoon, revealing her eagerness to start redesigning the garden immediately. Her letter continued, 'tomorrow and Thursday D[enis] M[itchell] and Keith [Leonard] could break the soil ready for Priaulx and I to plant over Xmas', concluding, 'I think my back isn't equal to digging therefore it would help to have K and DM' and 'I thought I might 'phone Tresidder [a local plant nursery] for plants almost at once.'[8]

Hepworth had been planning the garden for some time, and Rainier, who shared her belief in the revitalising, calming influence of nature, offered to help. They had organised musical and arts events together in St Ives, and although Rainier spent most of the year teaching in London she visited Hepworth often during the holidays. Both, too, were acquainted with men who had major horticultural interests. Hepworth had known Will Arnold-Forster since his intervention in the public-garden controversy in 1948. On visits to his home, Eagles Nest, set high on the hills above Zennor village, Hepworth would have been impressed by the marvellous garden he had created. She owned a copy of his classic book *Shrubs for the Milder Counties*, which had been published by Country Life Books in 1948.[9] Reading this and observing the wild plants about her, Hepworth's thoughts about gardening on this coastal fringe of Cornwall would have been confirmed; mild winters and the warming effects of the Gulf Stream were balanced by the bite of salt-laden winds that only the toughest plants could survive. Rainier had known the plant-hunting Viscount Chaplin of Totnes since they were music students together. His travels had included botanical expeditions to New Guinea; the planting ideas Rainier had assimilated from his estate and her familiarity with the plants of her native South Africa may have added to the range of plants Hepworth considered for Trewyn Studio. Hepworth also visited the Isles of Scilly and enjoyed the sub-tropical planting schemes established there from the 1850s, which illustrated how successful adventurous gardening plans could be.

Hepworth's copy of *Shrubs for the Milder Counties* has passages underlined in pencil and notes added in the margins beside certain plant descriptions. Tucked inside the front cover are two sheets of notepaper bearing Hepworth's distinctive handwriting. They appear to be a 'shopping list' for plants she was considering for Trewyn Studio, and many of these plants still flourish in the garden today.

Heading the first sheet is a list of the trees already present: 'Dracaena – 7 or 8 very large, Copper Beech, Holly, 2 pear trees, 2 or 3 elm (severely lopped)'. Beneath this is a note stating that the County Council had agreed to plant deciduous trees 'right up to Richmond Place', which formed part of the boundary between the public and private gardens. Scattered over the rest of this sheet and the next are the names of trees and shrubs being considered including *Hoheria sextylosa*, *Myrtus luma*, one large rowan tree, one magnolia (*grandiflora*), mimosa, eucalyptus and *Magnolia stellata*. The telephone number for Tresidder Nursery is noted and circled, and an interesting feature is that the current prices of some trees are included.

Work on remaking the garden started over Christmas 1956 – Rainier recalled that she and Hepworth had decided that the garden, which was heart-shaped with rose beds, 'needed a straight line of turf to give it form and distance'.[10] Denis Mitchell and Keith Leonard almost certainly did most of the digging, as Hepworth suffered intermittently from backaches. Turf, brought from a nearby building site, replaced the old lawn, but some of the roses were retained to be planted in two freshly cut, straight beds. The shallow pond was cleaned and reconstructed, and a decorative stone rockery added above it. Winter was not the ideal

Barbara Hepworth standing beside *Biolith* at Trewyn in 1949, with *Two Figures* in the foreground

MIRANDA PHILLIPS

View of Trewyn Studio garden in spring,
with *Torso II (Torcello)* in the foreground

season in which to replant, but fortunately there were no severe frosts that year and very few plants seemed to suffer adversely.

Over the next five or six years, extra plants were added: the Chusan or Chinese fan palm (*Trachycarpus fortunei*), the *Magnolia grandiflora* that shades the carving studio, *Fatsia japonica*, two hibiscus, a fuchsia hedge for shelter, a bay tree and the New Zealand satin flower (*Libertia grandiflora*). Two varieties of honeysuckle were set to sprawl over the rockery beside the pond and the lovely, scented water hawthorn (*Aponogeton distachyos*) planted to blossom in it. In summer the ultramarine and purple daisyheads of *Cineraria cruenta* bloomed and self-seeded, roses scented the air and tall blue agapanthus flowered. The garden paths meandered, presenting new views at every turn. The changing light conditions enhanced the sculptures that Hepworth had placed on breezeblock plinths amongst the flowers and foliage. The small, white-painted summerhouse was another addition – a place to relax and enjoy the peace of the garden, the bustle of the town temporarily forgotten.

In 1959 Barbara Hepworth approached John Milne to discuss buying a section of his garden, a move that would give her more space to display her work. A letter dated February 1959 enclosed her sketch-map, showing an addition of 3 feet 6 inches (1.06 metres) in depth on the south side of the garden, deepening to approximately 9 feet (2.75 metres) on the opposite edge, adjacent to the carving studio. A greenhouse, occasionally used by Milne as an extra studio, was included, as were two trees, a holly and a pear. The sale was not finalised until August 1965, probably as a result of the overriding need to work and exhibit, and the fact that Milne spent part of most years abroad. The new boundary, in spite of the delay, was agreed almost exactly along the line that Hepworth had sketched in 1959. This new section was cleared of its overgrown shrubbery and planted with *Pittosporum*, spotted laurel and *Berberis* varieties, as contrasts of form and colour. Several favourite sculptures were placed at strategic viewpoints in this woodland atmosphere. The greenhouse enabled Hepworth to grow plants that were too tender to grow outside. Plumbago and a cerise bougainvillea scrambled up the inner wall, whilst agave, aloe and even a few cacti shared shelves and the red-tiled floor.[11]

Barbara Hepworth with the art critic Mervyn Levy at Trewyn in 1962, with *Garden Sculpture (Model for Meridian)* in the foreground

In 1967 a fall on holiday in the Isles of Scilly resulted in a fractured hip that restricted Hepworth to a wheelchair for several months; thereafter she often used a walking stick for support. Some of the long recovery period was spent planning subtle changes in the garden. Photographs taken in the spring of 1969 show the main pathway bordered with stately white tulips, a gift from Holland. Unlike the small stone bridge that her assistants constructed over the pond, these tulips were temporary additions – Hepworth felt they were too formal for her essentially 'natural' garden. In early autumn that year, Hepworth and her old friend, the potter Bernard Leach, were awarded the Freedom of the Borough of St Ives and created Bards of the Cornish Gorsedd – extraordinary honours for citizens who were not Cornish natives.[12] As a response Hepworth opened Trewyn Studio garden to the people of St Ives, the first time that the public had seen this cloistered space. From time to time a writer or admirer was personally invited to tea in the garden, when Hepworth would urge them to 'Wander round the garden alone. Let them [the sculptures] look at you and they'll speak to you',[13] but it was usually Hepworth's domain, with her family, staff and cats the only visitors. The garden would have been particularly lovely for the public opening, with drifts of white Japanese anemones surrounding the late roses, and dark-blue and purple cinerarias providing contrasting colours and forms.[14] The upper part of the garden had honeysuckle and the first crinums' pink-flushed white trumpets; amongst the shrubs at the top of the garden were sprays of vibrant orange crocosmia and young spikes of berries on the Lords and Ladies (*Arum italicum*). The flowers and foliage both emphasised and provided counterpoint to the forms of Hepworth's sculptures.

[11] The majority of the cacti in the greenhouse belonged to one of Hepworth's assistants, Norman Stocker. When moving house he had nowhere to keep them; Hepworth offered to look after them temporarily, but they were never collected. As she already owned several these new additions were much enjoyed

[12] The Freedom of St Ives was awarded for Hepworth's contribution to the town in civic, as well as artistic, terms : she was an active member of the St Ives Trust, which acted to preserve St Ives' historic and architectural heritage, she had been a founder member of Cornwall County Council's 'Art in Schools' programme, and had given sculptures to the town. Hepworth's Bardic name was 'Gravyor' (Sculptor)

[13] M. Williams, newspaper article, 1988

[14] The deep red hybrid tea rose near the Chusan Palm was given to the garden in memory of the daughter of a friend of Sarah Bowness

As the number of sculptures that Hepworth wanted to keep close to her increased through the later 1960s, the lower half of the garden began to look overcrowded. Lack of space to display two large bronze groups, *The Family of Man* (1970) and *Conversation with Magic Stones* (1973), prompted her to write to Milne again. Hepworth successfully negotiated an additional slice of land, adding about 9 feet (2.75 metres) at the top southern corner of the garden, which neatened the line drawn in 1965. It enclosed a fine, mature dawn redwood (*Metasequoia glyptostroboides*), a short yew hedge and several small areas of bamboo. These were replanted to make a glade around *Conversation with Magic Stones*, whose massive forms were delicately contrasted on the other side of a pathway by the

'In the contemplation of Nature
we are perpetually renewed,
our sense of mystery and our
imagination is kept alive,
and rightly understood, it gives
us the power to project into a
plastic medium some universal
or abstract vision of beauty.'

Barbara Hepworth, 1934 [17]

[15] *St Ives Times*, 1976 and 1977

[16] Hepworth kept up to four cats at any one time
while she lived at Trewyn Studio – they appear
in many of the archive photographs. She fitted
all of them with collars and bells, but it is
unlikely that this deterred them from hunting

[17] Barbara Hepworth, article in *Unit One: The
Modern Movement in English Architecture,
Painting and Sculpture*, ed. Herbert Read, London
1934; reproduced in *Barbara Hepworth:
A Pictorial Autobiography*, London 1970,
revised ed. 1978, p.30

slender, ethereal *Apollo* (1951). The breeze, whispering though the bamboo, makes this a peaceful, meditative spot.

Dame Barbara Hepworth died in 1975, leaving instructions about Trewyn Studio in her will. Her family and executors fulfilled her wish to turn the house and garden into the small museum that continues to fascinate so many visitors. Over 14,000 people visited during the first year.[15] The museum staff, all of whom had worked for Hepworth, cared for the garden for some years but lacked the horticultural expertise to maintain it under such pressure of numbers. In 1984 the nurseryman and gardener John Anderson offered his services. With a lifetime's experience and knowledge, and a sensitivity to the vision of Hepworth's garden, he painstakingly restored its beauty. The exceptionally cold winter of 1987 killed the two *Hoheria sextylosa* that Hepworth had planted and caused some of the cordylines and phormiums to die back to ground level, but judicious replanting filled such gaps. Anderson only added plants that maintained the mood of the garden – informal, natural and relaxed rather than clipped and regimented – and preferred the natural control of pests and weeds in place of chemical methods. Hepworth would have approved; from her earliest years at Trewyn Studio she had been keen to attract wildlife – nestboxes were installed, hopefully out of the reach of her pet cats.[16] Blackbirds, thrushes and finches, plus the occasional magpie or wagtail, still visit regularly, drawn by seeds, fruit, insects and the pond. Redwing have been winter visitors. The omnipresent St Ives herring gulls perch and nest on the Studio roof but they prefer more open areas so are rarely seen in the garden itself. The pond, shaded for much of the year by the strap-like leaves of the water hawthorn, is colonised by frogs and toads, which prey on insects throughout the garden. Hedgehogs often track through the foliage and across the lawn during the night.

In 1980 the Museum became the responsibility of the Tate, their first venture outside London. The garden has matured and developed over the years, and the practice of replacing like with like has continued. In recent years a few of the older trees that had become unsafe or diseased were removed; the saplings that took their places are already growing vigorously. The sheltering hedges on the eastern and southern boundaries are pruned annually to reveal the view that Hepworth enjoyed from her garden: the Church tower, the rooftops of the town and the serene sweep of St Ives Bay beyond.

Trewyn Studio
garden, 15 May 1969

Clematis montana

BELOW The Montana group of clematis are all climbers and can provide dense cover for a fence or look charmingly old-fashioned grown on a trellis or through a tree – a vigorous *Clematis montana* will swiftly cover a wide area. Their leaves are mid-green and divided into three leaflets, while the flowers are four-petalled and up to 3 inches (7.5 cm) across, and are a pale or blush pink – the flower colours are darker in warmer areas. Flowers are produced only on new growth, so the plants should be pruned each year as soon as flowering is over to allow new wood to form. The majority of clematis are hardy – a few are only half-hardy – and they prefer rich, well-drained soil with some shade at the roots, though the main body of the plant can be grown in shade or full sun.

Chaenomeles japonica Japanese quince

OPPOSITE This early-flowering deciduous shrub, often known by the old names japonica or cydonia, has bright scarlet flowers with rounded petals and prominent anthers, which appear in masses of small clusters from late February until April. Small apple-shaped, golden-yellow fruits develop very slowly during summer – when ripe they can be used to make quince jelly, but need protracted cooking to produce even a small quantity. Alternatively, add one or two to a fruit-bowl to perfume the whole room. The glossy, rounded, dark-green leaves are shed in autumn to reveal mahogany-coloured branches set with thick, spiky thorns. As a spreading shrub, japonica will form an attractive, fairly compact shape in open positions, with some pruning, and can also be trained against a wall. Fully hardy, it likes good drainage and prefers a sunny position, but will tolerate shade.

Narcissus White daffodil

ABOVE Although narcissi have been grown and developed in Cornwall for many decades, Hepworth chose to grow only one variety at Trewyn. This delicate, pure white flower, with its long slender trumpet and narrow petals, makes a subtle addition to the garden. Narcissus bulbs need well-drained sites, but soil type and position are not important. In general they should be planted in September to achieve the best results, and covered by 2 to 4 inches (5 to 10 cm) of soil depending on bulb size. Like most bulbs, they benefit from a sprinkling of silver sand in the bottom of the planting hole. Be sure to remove flowers as they fade to prolong flowering, but let the foliage die back naturally until June or July to nourish the bulbs.

Four Square (Walk Through)
1966

Hepworth's wish for the spectator to engage physically with sculpture reached its full realisation in this work, which invites us to pass through its middle. The circular apertures lighten the form and offer shifting views into and out of the sculpture. Despite the geometric structure, each vertical element and each hole is irregular in shape. Hepworth acknowledged that her desire to make such large works sprang from a sense of urgency caused by the diagnosis of cancer in 1965. This piece replaced a rose bed that once occupied the same position.

prune hard to the desired size after they reach about 4 feet (1.2 metres) and have flowered once. Faded blooms should be removed to prolong flowering. They are frost-tender and will not tolerate temperatures below 5 °C (41 °F), but can be grown in large containers and moved into a cool greenhouse for winter. There are two brugmansias in the cold greenhouse at Trewyn – the classically lovely *Brugmansia suaveolens* 'Angel's trumpets', with its pendent, trumpet-shaped white blossoms, and *Brugmansia sanguinea* (illustrated here), with its slightly smaller orange-burgundy flowers.

Two Forms (Divided Circle)
1969

These delicately poised forms have a dramatic quality: the viewer is both invited to step through and denied access. Despite appearances, the sculpture is far from symmetrical, with the shapes of the two elements and their holes being very different (see page 13). As in *Four Square (Walk Through)*, the inside faces of the apertures were originally highly polished and golden in colour. The sinuous edges of these openings and the views they offer are important elements, introducing movement and space to the composition.

Brugmansia sanguinea Orange datura

ABOVE Originally from Mexico and South America, brugmansias were introduced on Tresco, Isles of Scilly, in the 1890s and still flourish outdoors there. Members of the same genus as aubergines and potatoes, they are very toxic and should be planted out of reach of children and pets. All the usually available varieties are rather rangy and ungainly-looking plants, and are grown for their magnificent flowers, which are large, fragrant, and produced sporadically from mid-summer to late autumn. For a neater shape,

Euryops pectinatus

LEFT A member of the daisy family (*Compositae*), the name Euryops comes from the Greek and means 'large-eyed', while the Latin pectinatus, or comb-like, refers to the plant's deep-cut leaves. Euryops forms a dense, upright evergreen shrub, with leaves that are a deep green with a silvery bloom. It carries bright yellow daisy-like flowers on 4 to 6 inch (10 to 15 cm) stems from early February until July, and often gives a second flush in autumn. Hardy to 5–7 °C (41–5 °F), it likes a sunny, fairly moist, but well-drained position. Euryops hate root disturbance and are best propagated by softwood cuttings in the summer.

Camellia japonica

RIGHT AND OPPOSITE Originally from China and Japan, camellias are named after the chemist Georg Josef Kamel (1661–1706), who made a lifetime study of the flora of the Philippines and the Far East. They are outstandingly beautiful plants – most form dense, upright bushes with crisp, glossy, dark-green leaves and delicate blooms. The flowers vary from an almost luminous white, through shades (and even streaks) of pink and red, to deepest claret. Forms range from the simplest of singles to complex peony forms and doubles. Most varieties are hardy and can be grown outdoors; however they do flower early, and buds can be damaged by frost or cold winds, which should be considered when choosing a planting site. Camellias also require an acid, lime-free soil – where the soil is alkaline or neutral, they can be grown in containers in a good lime-free compost. Pruning is only necessary to retain a neat shape and should be done after flowering.

Cineraria cruenta 'Stellata'

LEFT Cineraria is best known as the brightly flowered, compact houseplant, *Cineraria multiflora*, which can make showy displays in an unheated greenhouse but is not really suitable for garden use. This strain was developed over many years from *Cineraria cruenta*, a native of the Canary Islands with attractive foliage and flowers. Cruenta is a perennial but is best treated as an annual by raising new plants from seed each year. This is remarkably easy: just collect the ripe, downy seedheads that form when the flowers have withered, sow them in open ground in February to April and rake in lightly, or just allow the plant to self seed. Clusters of the daisy-like flowers are produced throughout the summer in a variety of colours – mid-blue, deep indigo, violet or claret – with a centre that is a deeper shade of the petal colour. Poor and stony soil conditions are no obstacle, but the plant will benefit from well-drained soil and slight shade.

Cantate Domino
1958

The title of this work – 'O Sing unto the Lord' in Latin – is the opening line of Psalm 98, and reflects Hepworth's renewed spirituality following the death of her son, Paul, in 1953. While its form may suggest hands clasped in prayer, the rising movement of the composition seems celebratory. There is also the suggestion of organic growth, as the bronze appears to unfold out of the lower section like an emerging seedling. This combination of spirituality and nature is typical of the artist.

they age. Although it flowers for a relatively short period, the cherry is enchanting for those two or three weeks – a perfect foil to the blue-green patina of Hepworth's bronzes. Unusually, the euonymus 'Silver Queen' has been grown up through the cherry, and its variegated cream-bordered foliage stands as a contrast to the cherry bark. Euonymus is an excellent shrub for seaside gardens, resisting salt-laden winds admirably and thriving even in sandy soils.

Allium triquetrum Three-cornered leek

RIGHT This pretty member of the onion family is native to the western Mediterranean and is generally known as three-cornered leek, or stinking garlic. It was introduced to Cornwall in 1752 for garden cultivation by returning seamen, but rapidly became established along roadsides and in churchyards. Although only recorded in Devon nearly a century later, it has now spread throughout most of southern Britain. The bright green leaves start to appear before Christmas and can be distinguished from narcissus leaves by their triangular cross section, with its well-defined 'keel'. When the plant is bruised or broken it releases an overwhelming smell of crushed raw garlic, so, despite its spike of attractive, drooping, white-bell flowers, it is unsuitable as a cut flower. A tough, invasive specimen, it is not available commercially – you will have to find a gardener who is willing to divide a clump if you wish to grow it.

Geranium maderense

BELOW *Geranium maderense* takes up to four years to reach flowering size. During this time it produces large, glossy, deeply lobed and toothed leaves, which are dark green and carried on stiff, red-tinted stems, radiating from a woody central stem. By the third or fourth year the plant should look as if it has been trained to a 'standard' shape, although it may be rather top heavy. By its fourth year the geranium should be mature enough to flower, but will need a long, hot, sunny summer to produce worthwhile blooms.

If conditions are right, a spherical cluster of sticky-haired, pinkish-grey stems and buds will form above the central rosette of leaves. The buds burst into rich, vibrant magenta flowers. The petals have a satin sheen, and their colour is the ideal counterpoint to the leaves. Seedheads can be left on the plant to mature, but, once they are ripe (or have emptied), should be removed. Apart from its fickle flowering habits, this is a trouble-free plant and, though demanding full sun, will tolerate any well-drained soil.

Torso II (Torcello) 1958

This is one of a series of three works suggesting both the human torso and a single bone. Among Hepworth's most organic forms, these all have sub-titles with marine or Mediterranean associations. Torcello is an island in the Venetian lagoon that is renowned for its Byzantine basilicas and mosaics, which Hepworth had visited. The artist photographed all three 'torsos' against the sea, and it may be significant that she sited this piece in the garden close to water.

Euonymus radicans 'Silver Queen' and Prunus 'Kanzan' Japanese cherry

ABOVE There are many varieties of flowering cherry, and Hepworth's is probably 'Kanzan', as it is strongly recommended in her preferred gardening book. Usually breaking into flower at the end of April, it is smothered in bloom through the first fortnight of May, leaving the lawn at Trewyn strewn with a confetti of shed flowers. The pendent, fully double blooms are a delicate pink, fading almost to white as

Zantedeschia aethiopica 'Crowborough'

BELOW   Also known as white arum lily and lily of the Nile, this dramatic perennial likes well-drained soil but also grows well in up to 6 inches (15 cm) of water as a marginal pond plant. Originally from South Africa, it is hardy and evergreen in mild areas such as Cornwall, but needs a minimum temperature of 10 °C (50 °F) so should be planted in movable containers or a cold greenhouse in chillier areas. It forms clumps of arrowhead-shaped leaves about 10 inches (25 cm) long that grow to a height of about 2 feet (60 cm). The rich green leaves, and later the showy white flowers on the stems above them, unfurl in an echo of the fluid movement of the sculpture *Corymb* so close to them. 'Crowborough', the variety shown here, is virginally white with a pale-yellow spathe – black-throated, pink and yellow varieties are readily available.

Solanum crispum 'Glasnevin'

ABOVE   Generally known as the potato vine, and from the same genus as the potato, this perennial is grown for its loose clusters of small star-shaped flowers. A scrambler rather than a true climber, it is best trained up and through a bush or a trellis. It has small, dark-green, pointed oval leaves, which are occasionally divided into lobes at the base, and mauve blooms with prominent clusters of bright yellow stamens, which flower from midsummer until October or November. Solanum is half-hardy and semi-evergreen, requiring a sunny position in fertile, well-drained soil to produce the best blooms.

Corymb 1959

Hepworth's use of nature as a source for her art is especially clear in this work. A corymb is a floral cluster in which the buds are borne on long stems that rise from a single, unbranched stalk, giving a flat head of flowers. As the sculpture is not consistent with that definition, it seems likely that Hepworth wished simply to conjure up a general idea of inflorescence. Her positioning of the work amongst the flowers and foliage of the garden reinforces the association.

Argyranthemum frutescens
Marguerite

RIGHT This hardy, attractive perennial is rapidly gaining popularity as a containerised plant, but can be better appreciated in open ground. Usually known as the marguerite or Paris daisy, it is another of the Trewyn plants that originated in the Canary Islands, so is best suited to a well-drained soil and a sunny position. A first-year marguerite will grow to one foot (30 cm) or so and will produce many of its daisy-like white flowerheads from late April until September, aided by regular 'dead heading' of old blooms. The finely divided, fern-like leaves are evergreen, and, as the plant grows, the stems will take on the appearance of a trunk. After four years the marguerite will, with care and pruning, be a bushy shape, smothered in flowers all summer. It can reach a height of 3 feet (90 cm) and may need support if it becomes top heavy.

River Form 1965, cast 1973

Like many of Hepworth's bronzes, this was cast from a wood carving. The interiors of these were often painted and the contrast of outer and inner surfaces was echoed in her patination of the bronze. It was, perhaps, the horizontality of the sculpture and the eddy-like spiralling of its holes that suggested the title. In the garden at Trewyn, the collecting of rainwater within the sculpture adds an extra dimension which is especially appropriate to the title.

Astilbe

ABOVE A member of the saxifrage family, astilbes can vary from 8 inches (20 cm) to 4 feet (120 cm) high, in shades from white through pinks to a deep carmine. They have broad leaves divided into oval, deeply toothed leaflets, which are usually deep green but sometimes flushed with bronze. Elegant, feathery panicles of tiny star-shaped blooms are carried well above the foliage on slender stems. Occasionally known as Prince of Wales' feathers, these work well as cut blooms both alone or as part of a larger arrangement. Astilbes prefer moist, partly shaded sites, but can perform well in drier, sunnier spots, and benefit from an annual spring mulch of well-rotted compost. They can be propagated by careful division in spring or autumn, or grown from ripened seed, and, as the flower spikes are attractive when dried brown in winter, it is worth leaving a few when the plant finishes flowering for this purpose.

Abutilon pictum 'Thompsonii'

BELOW Of the three abutilon varieties at Trewyn, this one attracts most compliments. Trained up a white-washed brick wall in the cold greenhouse, its beautiful vine-shaped leaves are displayed to perfection. Pictum means painted, and the leaves are bright green, heavily speckled with a rich pale yellow, up to 7 inches (18 cm) long and 5 inches (12.5 cm) wide. The soft apricot-coloured flowers are an incurved bell shape, pendent, and veined with crimson, but they are often hidden amongst the abundant foliage. At Trewyn, pictum blooms from May to July, often with a small second flush in late August. It can be grown in a sheltered spot outside in warmer areas and can tolerate temperatures as low as 7 °C (45 °F) but could be vulnerable to a cold snap. Like the other varieties at Trewyn – *Abutilon megapoticum* and *Abutilon vitifolium* – this one can be tip pruned in spring to encourage bushy growth and old branches cut back hard, and it needs fertile, well-drained soil along with sun or dappled shade.

Bougainvillea glabra Paper flower

ABOVE Bougainvilleas, named after the scientist and explorer Louis de Bougainville (1729–1811), are tender climbers. Glabra is a semi-evergreen that retains the majority of its dark-green, oval leaves in temperatures above 10 °C (50 °F). Although too tender to grow outdoors, bougainvilleas flourish even in cold greenhouses, rapidly reaching heights of 20 feet (6 metres) and a similar spread, requiring a trellis in their second or third year of growth. They like fertile, well-drained soil and a lot of light – the more sun the plant gets the more brilliant its showy magenta 'flowers'. These are really floral bracts, like those of a poinsettia, but provide a colourful background for the true bloom – a tiny cream structure. The bracts, which look as delicate as tissue paper, are borne throughout the summer and well into autumn, but last only a day or two if cut for arrangements. There are many other species with vibrant colours available – reds, yellows, pinks and purples – though they are not easy to find and most of them need higher temperatures than glabra.

Sea Form (Porthmeor)

This is the plaster from which an edition of seven bronzes was cast. It may have been painted this bronze-like colour when exhibited in St Ives Guildhall in 1968. The title refers to a nearby beach, known for its long waves rolling in from the Atlantic. While the curled edges of the sculpture echo the form of a turning wave, the patination seems to emulate the colour of the sea. More generally, the sculpture's irregularity, expansive form and ambiguous space recreate aspects of the natural realm.

Cordyline australis Australian cabbage palm

BELOW Also known as the New Zealand cabbage tree, this palm is named from the Greek 'kordyle' – a club – referring to the large, fleshy roots of some varieties. It is also known as the dracaena, and smaller varieties are often sold as potted plants. Semi-hardy and evergreen, palms can tolerate temperatures down to about 10 °C (50 °F). A cordyline in a favourable position in open ground can reach 40 feet (12 metres) or more, with the 'topknot' of leaves spreading to 15 feet (4.5 metres). The oldest of the sword-shaped leaves wither and are shed in late autumn to free the plant's resources for the next season's growth. Stiff, branched panicles up to 3 feet (90 cm) long, which tend to spoil the plant's symmetry, carry the small, heavily scented, creamy flowers in mid-summer; these are followed by a mass of spherical fruits. The fruit branches can be removed if desired, as they add weight to the top of plant.

Fuchsia magellanica

ABOVE Named after the German physician and herbalist Leonard Fuchs (1506–1566), the fuchsia was originally a southern-hemisphere plant but has been extensively developed since its introduction to Britain in 1800. The hardiest form, magellanica, is easily propagated, very wind tolerant, and forms attractive hedges, especially if regularly cut hard back. A fuchsia hedge will filter the wind more effectively than a solid windbreak, helping to prevent turbulence inside the garden. Magellanica has adapted so well that it is now a common hedgerow addition in Cornwall, the Isle of Man and parts of Ireland. It has small dark-green leaves, which are reddish when young, and it is strung with pairs of garnet and purple flowers from April to November. In colder areas it should be cut to the ground before the frost can cause damage – it will spring back vigorously the following season. Hybrid fuchsias are generally less hardy but come in an ever-increasing variety of flower types and colours, many resembling icing-sugar decorations – some will undoubtedly perform better under glass.

Stone Sculpture (Fugue II) 1956

For Hepworth, the form of a sculpture was dictated by the material from which it was carved, and she wrote of the sculptor's search for the work's 'structure of rhythm'. Comparisons of sculpture with music were common for her, as the title of this work indicates. The limestone of *Stone Sculpture* is characterised by numerous fossils. Originally, the stone was more highly finished, but long display outside has weathered its surface.

Autumn

Roses

According to her family and friends, roses were Barbara Hepworth's favourite flowers, and her first garden at Trewyn was almost entirely planted with them. As the garden developed and evolved, other plants were introduced to add variety and a longer flowering time. Today roses remain a favourite at Trewyn, whether floribundas, some red and one orange hybrid teas, even a couple of species roses which are left unpruned after flowering to develop their scarlet fruits for the garden birds. One of Hepworth's gardening books contains a receipt for the lovely, slightly scented hybrid tea, 'Alexander'; another hybrid tea in a deep velvety crimson was planted as a memorial to a family friend.

The variety of roses at Trewyn makes it difficult to specify all their individual requirements, but a few basic guidelines can be followed. Most roses are hardy, prefer open, sunny positions, and need shelter from salt-laden or strong winds. The soil should be moist, fertile and well drained, and the rose should be fed in winter or early spring to ensure high-quality blooms. Pruning varies according to type and sometimes to the gardener's preference. Try not to plant in areas where roses have been grown in the last five years to avoid the effects of the harmful soil organisms that can blight new plants.

Sphere with Inner Form 1963

Sculptures in which one small form is enclosed within another larger one had been common in Hepworth's work since the 1930s. She drew attention to the relationship between inside and outside: 'a nut in its shell or of a child in the womb, or in the structure of shells or of crystals'. These works, then, evoke a sense of growth, nurture and protection. While this reflects Hepworth's common use of natural forms and processes, such concerns have been specifically related to her particular view as a woman and a mother.

Phyllostachys 'Henonis' Bamboo

ABOVE East Asian in origin, phyllostachys bamboos are clump forming and evergreen, and can provide an attractive screen dividing the garden into sections. Bamboo is an increasingly popular plant, of which there are many varieties available – most of these like rich, light, moist soils. All bamboos die after flowering, which fortunately only happens once every thirty or forty years. Thus, if a bamboo does flower, it is important to save seed. The only pruning required is the cutting down of tired-looking old stems, which should be cut right down to ground level, but can then be used as supports for other plants. According to variety, phyllostachys bamboos can grow from 6 feet (1.8 metres) to 25 feet (7.5 metres), and will spread as far as you let them. They need a sheltered position as they can be badly damaged by wind. Other types of bamboo will offer differing growth patterns – it is possible to find one suitable for most gardens.

Yucca gloriosa

LEFT Yuccas come from the southern United States, Mexico and the Caribbean, and were originally thought to be members of the cassava family – yucca is the Caribbean word for cassava. They have many common names including Adam's Needle and Spanish Bayonet, and were introduced by Augustus Smith to his sub-tropical gardens on Tresco in 1857, probably from Kew Gardens in London. Yuccas look exotic but are fully hardy. Stiff, blue-grey, sword-shaped leaves are carried in a rosette above a short, stout stem. The leaf tips are formidably sharp, and the rosette of leaves can reach a height of 2 to 3 feet (60 to 90 cm). During the summer a tall flower stalk develops from the centre of the rosette, which will bear up to 40 pendent tulip-shaped flowers in the autumn. These are creamy white, flushed with a dusky red on the outside. The flower spike should be cut back when spent, leaving only about 2 inches (5 cm) above the leaves. Yuccas take about three years to become established, can be grown in large containers or open ground, like any well-drained soil, and enjoy full sun or light shade. Among the most valuable 'architectural' plants, they look best on their own or in clusters of up to three.

> ### Conversation with Magic Stones 1973
>
> This was Hepworth's last major bronze. Despite ill health, she was able to oversee the positioning of each piece. Though apparently abstract, the vertical element suggest figures. Their inter-relationship stands as a metaphor for human inter-action, while a tension is established between them an the smaller stones, which may be seen as embodiments of metaphysical or magical forces. The group has also been compared with the circles of standing stones tha can be seen in the landscape close to St Ives.

Pelargoniums

RIGHT Bred from several South African species, pelargoniums are frost-tender and will not tolerate temperatures below 0 °C (32 °F). Usually grown in pots in the home, conservatory or greenhouse, they are, however, extremely easy to propagate from cuttings, so it is simple to raise new stock every winter to bed out for summer. They come in a huge range of sizes and in every shade of pink from clear white to dark, velvety burgundy. Most have a long flowering season, and quickly sprout new growth if pruned. *Pelargonium hortorum* and scented-leaf varieties are the best to bed out in the garden – at Trewyn there are hortorums in vivid scarlet and white, and the lemon-scented 'Mabel Grey', which all overwinter successfully most years but may not survive in chilly areas. *Pelargonium peltatum* is ivy-leaved and best suited to hanging baskets and window boxes. *Pelargonium domesticum*, or regals, are perhaps least suited to outdoor use, but make excellent house or conservatory specimens.

Solanum jasminoides 'Album'

RIGHT Like 'Glasnevin' (see page 28), 'Album' is a perennial, but flowers rather later. Its white blooms continue well into December – at Trewyn it can even produce clusters of flowers in January in mild years. Crowded stems can be pruned out in spring, and both varieties can be started from ripened seed in spring or from semi-ripe cuttings in summer.

Mahonia japonica

OPPOSITE Collected by the 'plant hunter' Robert Fortune in China in the 1840s, *Mahonia japonica* is an evergreen shrub with rosettes of deep-green shiny and spiky leaves, and forms a rather dense shape. It eventually reaches a height of about 7 feet (2 metres) and a similar spread. It filters wind effectively, but its true value is apparent just before Christmas when the rosettes of flower spikes, often 6 inches (15 cm) long, begin to open. Delicate lemon-yellow flowers brighten the mahonia from December to late February; their scent carries well and always intrigues visitors to Trewyn. A small spray of flowers will perfume a room, though petals are shed rapidly. The berries that follow are a deep purple-blue and are much loved by birds, particularly the occasional brambling overwintering in Cornwall. Mahonias are fully hardy, preferring shade or semi-shade and fertile, well-drained but not dry soil.

Coré
1955–6,
cast 1960

The white
marble carving
from which this
piece was cast
once stood in a
similar position
in the garden.
That original
material is,
perhaps, better
suited to the
work's title,
which is a type
of ancient Greek
female figure
sculpture. Its
organic curves,
however, are
very different
to the rigid
verticality of
such antique
objects. Though
the arc and
circle near the
top may suggest
a face, they may
also refer to the
sun and moon,
standing as
fundamental
forces of nature.

Aucuba japonica **'Variegata'**
Spotted laurel and berries

ABOVE A handsome evergreen shrub with large, pointed oval leaves, laurel thrives almost anywhere, even in deep shade under trees or in city areas. 'Variegata' is one of the most valuable forms – its glossy, rich green leaves are heavily speckled with a sharp yellow. The flowers, blooming through March and April, are small and insignificant, but a female

variety is capable of bearing attractive oval red berries in small clusters from autumn through winter if a male laurel is within pollinating distance. To cover a large, shady patch of garden and ensure the maximum show of berries, plant three females to each male. Spotted laurel forms a rounded bush from 6 to 10 feet (1.8 to 3 metres) in height and spread, and should succeed in any garden soil.

Fatsia japonica

BELOW LEFT Also known as the false castor oil plant, this evergreen shrub looks remarkably exotic in an English garden. It carries globe-shaped clusters of small, creamy white flowers from September to November, followed by dull green berries that turn matt black as winter progresses. The dark, glossy green leaves are deeply lobed and often more than one foot (30 cm) across. Fatsia is perhaps best known as a houseplant but fares (and looks) better when allowed to reach its full height – 10 feet (3 metres) or so – amongst other plants. It likes well-drained, fertile soil, and tolerates full sun, though preferring partial shade. It needs shelter from strong winds in colder districts, but thrives in the south and west of England, and is completely frost hardy. Pruning is only necessary if the plant is crowding its neighbours or looking ungainly, and should be carried out in spring.

Hibiscus syriacus **'Bluebird'**

RIGHT Native to China and Japan, *Hibiscus syriacus* was first collected in Syria, hence its name. A deciduous shrub, it reaches 10 feet (3 metres) in height and, eventually, a similar spread. It is late to leaf – often well into May – but the stems remain an attractive buff until then. The deeply lobed leaves are a fresh lime-green when they first appear, maturing to a dark green. Abundant flowers open from July to October, each lasting only a day or two – they are not suitable for arrangements as they tend to drop after a few hours if cut. 'Bluebird', one of the most beautiful of the outdoor varieties, has open, trumpet-shaped flowers 3 to 4 inches (7 to 10 cm) across. The petals have a glossy sheen, and the blooms are a deep violet-blue with a dark crimson eye. Though much hardier than it looks, the hibiscus will not tolerate cold winds or a late frost. Generally, it needs full sun and a well-drained soil, and requires very little pruning – just cut back old or ungainly branches in the late spring.

Figure for Landscape

1959–60

The title of this work suggests that Hepworth may have imagined it sited in the countryside. She often referred to the importance of the figure in the landscape and to the relationship between the individual human body and the wider environment. In her work she sought to say something affirmative about this relationship, about being in the world. In reducing the figure to a simple, shrouded form she obscures any definite identity, allowing it to stand for everyone.

43

Hedera helix English ivy

BELOW   Although there are few species of ivy, there are innumerable varieties, many suitable for cultivation inside or outside. Although most are fully hardy, a few of the most delicate indoor plants are half-hardy. *Hedera helix* has the typical three to five lobed leaves, and will climb relentlessly up any obstacle. The stems are woody and produce short aerial roots from nodes; these attach themselves to suitable damp surfaces. Although usually found in shady positions, it climbs upwards in a constant pursuit of light – in dense shade, ivy produces longer, less branching stems with larger gaps between leaves to conserve energy. A moderately shady position with a good light source will encourage leafier, more attractive growth. Most ivies produce insignificant greenish-yellow flowers in these conditions, followed by dull black berries, which are a valuable food source for birds. Variegated ivies need more light than plain green varieties. Both benefit from occasional misting when inside, or even when outside if conditions are hot and dry. Cutting off growing tips will encourage side growth – ivy can be left to progress naturally or pruned as ruthlessly as desired in order to achieve a good shape.

Daphne odora **'Aureomarginata'**

ABOVE   *Daphne odora* is the most fragrant variety of a scented genus. 'Aureomarginata' refers to the narrow, creamy yellow margin around the glossy, dark-green leaves. A slow-growing evergreen, it forms a dense bushy shrub, eventually reaching a height and spread of 5 feet (1.5 metres). Small clusters of flowers start opening in January and often continue into April. Each bloom is a pale lilac-pink within and a deeper rose-purple on the outside. Their perfume drifts across the garden in the early spring and is heady, exotic and sweet – a couple of sprigs in a glass will scent a room. Daphnes need fertile, well-drained soil but must not be allowed to dry out at the roots – a leaf-mould mulch will help avoid this. All are frost hardy, some are fully hardy, and they all need full sun to produce the finest foliage and blossom, though will tolerate some shade.

Image

1951–2

As the title suggests, Hepworth wished this work to stand for a generalised identity. She related *Image* to the notion of the figure in the landscape, and described such figures as 'powerfully rooted' and as creating the impression of 'growth and expansion … an *image*, or symbol of the span of time'. Implicitly, she was comparing her work to the ancient monoliths of West Cornwall.

Euphorbia characias and *Euphorbia wulfenii*

BELOW Euphorbias are a huge genus – around fifteen varieties are native to Britain and Europe, with a range of evocative folk-names such as wolf's bane and purging spurge (a name indicating the genus's historical uses as both a purgative and a poison – waterproof gloves should always be worn when cutting or handling euphorbias). Characias is native to Greece and the Balkans, but has been cultivated in British gardens since the early 19th century. It is fully hardy and forms a clump of tough, upright stems 3 feet (90 cm) or more high, clothed in long, narrow, blue-green leaves, giving an effect rather like a fat, green, bottle-brush. Euphorbias flower from December until mid-June, but the flowers are insignificant. Like the poinsettia, they are valued for their flower bracts, which are a bright yellowish-green, cup-shaped, and form at the top of the stem. Characias will flower annually, producing bract and flowerheads up to 6 inches (15 cm) tall at the tip of the stems. Each bract is further enhanced by a dark burgundy centre within the cup. The subspecies flowers biennially and carries rather larger canary yellow 'flowerlets' within the bracts. All euphorbias self-seed vigorously, grow best in sun or partial shade and prefer a well-drained soil. Old stems that have finished flowering should be cut back to ground level after seeding, ensuring new plants next season.

Garden Sculpture (Model for Meridian) 1958

An intermediate stage in the development of the 15-feet (2.5 metres) high *Meridian* for a new building in London, the form of this sculpture evokes ideas of organic growth with which Hepworth hoped to relieve the stark geometry of the architecture. The sculpture was made in several sizes, the initial idea being fashioned from pipe-cleaners. Both the expanding forms and the highly textured surface suggest the natural associations made explicit by its title.

Cordyline australis
Australian
cabbage palm

One of the first plants
introduced by Augustus
Smith (1804–1872),
cordylines are now a
familiar feature of many
of Britain's seaside
resorts, making wonder-
fully impressive trees
that evoke memories of
idyllic summer holidays.
New plants can either be
started from suckers or
ripened seed in spring,
or taken from cuttings in
summer. Cuttings should
be taken from the stem,
cut to one-inch (2.5 cm)
lengths, planted horizon-
tally to half their depth
in sandy compost, and
kept at a temperature
of 18–21 °C (64–70 °F),
preferably with
bottom heat.

WINTER

Chronology

1903	Born 10 January in Wakefield, Yorkshire, the eldest of four children.
1920–4	Studies sculpture at Leeds School of Art and Royal College of Art, London.
1924–6	Travels in Italy. Marries sculptor John Skeaping in May 1925 in Florence, and the two study in Rome under the master-carver Ardini.
1926	November – returns to Britain and settles in St John's Wood, London.
1928	Moves to Mall Studios, Hampstead, where she remains until 1939. June – first one-person exhibition.
1929	Birth of a son, Paul.
1931	Meets the painter Ben Nicholson; they marry in 1938.
1932	Joint exhibition with Nicholson.
1933	Easter – Hepworth and Nicholson travel to Provence via Paris; they are invited to join the avant-garde group *Abstraction-Création*. Hepworth and Skeaping divorce. June – the founding of *Unit 1* secures Hepworth and Nicholson a place at the heart of a British avant-garde.
1934	October – birth of triplets.
1939	August – the family move to Carbis Bay, St Ives, Cornwall. Conditions are not good and Hepworth makes few sculptures for several years.
1943	First retrospective exhibition, Temple Newsam, Leeds.
1946	First post-war one-person exhibition, Alex. Reid & Lefevre, London.
1949	September – purchases Trewyn Studio.
1950	Visits the Venice Biennale where she represents Britain.
1951	Major work installed at Festival of Britain. Designs sets and costumes for Sophocles's *Electra*, Old Vic theatre, London. Hepworth and Nicholson divorce.
1954	Major retrospective, Whitechapel Art Gallery, London. Visit to Greece inspires a group of large hardwood sculptures. Designs sets and costumes for composer Michael Tippett's *Midsummer Marriage*, Covent Garden, London.
1955–6	Major exhibition tours North America.
1958	Hepworth is created CBE; Nicholson leaves St Ives.
1959	Exhibition at São Paulo Biennal wins Grand Prix and tours South America.
1963	*Single Form* is commissioned for the United Nations, New York.
1964–5	Major exhibition tours Europe.
1965	Made Dame of the British Empire.
1966	Diagnosed with cancer of the throat; the disease is successfully treated.
1968	Retrospective, Tate Gallery, London.
1975	Having continued to work despite increasing frailty, Hepworth dies in a studio fire on 20 May.

Further Reading

A.M. Hammacher, *Barbara Hepworth*, London 1968, rev. ed. 1987

Barbara Hepworth: A Pictorial Autobiography, London 1970, rev. ed. 1978

Sally Festing, *Barbara Hepworth: A Life of Forms*, Harmondsworth 1995

David Thistlewood (ed.), *Barbara Hepworth Reconsidered*, Liverpool 1996

Penelope Curtis, *St Ives Artists: Barbara Hepworth*, London 1998

Matthew Gale and Chris Stephens, *Barbara Hepworth: Works in the Tate Collection and the Barbara Hepworth Museum St Ives*, London 1999